D0174934

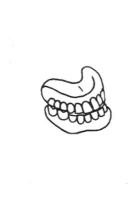

Created and published by Knock Knock
1635-B Electric Avenue
Venice, CA 90291
knockknockstuff.com

Illustrations by Gemma Correll

This book is a work of editorial nonfiction meant
solely for entertainment purposes. It is not
intended to create actual panic or serve as
psychological advice or counsel. In no event
will Knock Knock be liable to any reader for any
damages, including direct, indirect, incidental,
special, consequential, or punitive damages,
arising out of or in connection with the use
of the information contained in this book.
So there.

Every reasonable attempt has been made to
identify owners of copyright. Errors or omissions
will be corrected in subsequent editions.

ISBN: 978-160106577-3
UPC: 825703-50029-5

10 9 8 7

1.

You'll be over the hill.*

*Hey, you made it to the top.

2.

You'll have an endless list of aches and pains.*

*You'll never run out of things to talk about.

3.

You're too old to be a whiz kid.*

*You're never too old to reinvent yourself.

4.

Impromptu naps will be part of your daily routine.*

*And what's wrong with that?

5.

Life will get boring—and so will you.*

*No one can tame the beast inside you.

6.

You'll die alone.*

*There's always pet koi fish.
They can live to 200!

7.

Reading glasses will become a must-have accessory.*

*They'll make you look sophisticated.

8.

You won't have enough material to write a memoir.*

*You can publish an autobiographical pamphlet. Kids today have such short attention spans anyway.

9.

You'll mistake your new boss for an intern.*

10.

Your once cool tattoo will morph into something unrecognizable.*

*You can tell people it's Surrealist.

100 Reasons to Panic about Getting Old

KNOCK KNOCK®
VENICE, CALIFORNIA

11.

Hair will appear in places you don't want it.*

*At least you'll have hair!

12.

Hair will disappear from places you want to keep it.*

*You'll save on haircuts.

13.

You won't get into cool clubs anymore.*

*You'll get into the AARP.

14.

You'll have to supersize your pill case.*

*You can impress other old people with it.

15.

When younger people say "ma'am" or "sir," they'll mean you.*

*At least those darn kids have some manners.

16.

You'll no longer care about the hipness of restaurants.*

*It's freeing, isn't it?

17.

You'll get stuck living in a retirement community.*

*It'll be like summer camp—for old people!

18.

Your joints will
be creaky.*

*People will always know
when you're in the room.

19.

Plastic-encased furniture will feature prominently in your decor.*

*It'll be easy to wipe up spills.

20.

You'll be accused of being a bad driver.*

*You can run over your critics
with your giant boat of a car.

21.

You won't be a regular at the corner bar anymore.*

*You'll be on a first-name basis with the pharmacist.

22.

You'll go bald.*

*Less hair means less maintenance.

23.

Potential suitors will be scared off by all your cats.*

*Who needs a suitor? You've got a ton of cats.

24.

Your kids will end up hating you.*

*Or loving you a whole lot.

25.

Colonoscopies will become a regular thing.*

*You'll finally know what your insides look like.

26.

You won't get carded anymore.*

*And you won't have to reveal your age to the bouncer.

27.

One glass of wine will give you a hangover.*

*Your liver will thank you.

28.

If you date a younger woman, people will think you're her dad.*

*You can make her order off the kids' menu.

29.

If you date a
younger man,
people will call
you a cougar.*

*Cougars are fierce predators.

30.

Two words:
hot flashes.*

*You'll have an excuse for mood swings.

31.

You'll become
a little blue
pill popper.*

*Hello, endurance!

32.

You'll misplace your glasses. The ones that you're wearing on top of your head.*

*Old and forgetful go together like peanut butter and jelly.

33.

Your hair will turn gray.*

*You'll have a better base to dye it blue.

34.

You'll trade in your motorcycle for a mobility scooter.*

*Yeah, but you can't ride a chopper through the mall.

35.

They don't make cars—or toasters, or robots—like they used to.*

*You're going to die soon, so you won't have to keep replacing them.

36.

You'll get a hideous recliner.*

*When you drift off while watching the six o'clock news, you'll be comfortable.

37.

You won't be up on current music.*

*Whatever it is, you'll just call it a racket anyway.

38.

You'll turn into a frail geriatric.*

*You can guilt people into doing
all the heavy lifting for you.

39.

All your friends will die before you.*

*You'll make new friends.
These ones won't know your past.

40.

You'll die before all your friends.*

*At least you won't be lonely.

41.

Your cool vintage clothes will just look like old clothes on you.*

*You can overcharge hipsters
for the contents of your closets.

42.

You'll have to plan your own funeral.*

*You'll plan something to make a Viking proud.

43.

Your skin will sag.*

*You can put a plastic surgeon's
kid through college.

44.

Plastic surgery will make you look like a wax figure.*

*It's better than sagging skin.

45.

Dentures?
Yikes.*

*Dentures pulled out =
instant Halloween costume!

46.

Incontinence? Yikes.*

*Adult diapers mean never
having to hold it again.

47.

Polyester will be a major part of your wardrobe.*

*It's so easy to launder!

48.

You'll only
be able to eat
bland food.*

*Mush: it's what's for dinner.
And breakfast. And lunch.

49.

You'll tell kids to get off your lawn.*

*You'll also tell them how you used to walk to school uphill in the snow, both ways.

50.

Your big night out will be an early bird special and senior tickets to the movies.*

*You'll be a cheap date.

51.

You'll write
angry letters
to the editor.*

*Better that than yelling at people in person.

52.

Your free time
will be spent
playing golf.*

*You'll have an excuse to wear crazy plaid pants.

53.

You'll start talking to yourself.*

*Take up gardening—plants love to be talked to.

54.

You'll have a midlife crisis and cling to your youth.*

*At least you're going down fighting.

55.

They'll take away your license.*

*You can hire a chauffeur
to cart you around. Fancy!

56.

Your nest egg
won't last.*

*Those senior discounts will come in handy.

57.

You'll never do a cartwheel again.*

*You can join a senior tap-dancing group.

58.

Your favorite vacations will be cruises.*

*Those all-you-can-eat buffets are delicious.

- -

59.

Fertility will be a thing of the past.*

*You'll no longer have to
worry about birth control.

- -

60.

Your finger won't be on the pulse of fashion or trends.*

*You'll know what's new
in the world of arthritis medications.

61.

When you die, your loved ones will find your diary— and read it.*

*Who cares—you'll be long gone!

62.

Lying about your age is wrong, but it will feel so right.*

*Forty is the new thirty. Fifty is the new forty.
Sixty is the new fifty. And so on . . .

63.

Your once smooth skin will become wrinkled.*

*They're not wrinkles, they're life lines.

64.

You'll die a horrible death.*

*Nah, it'll probably be heart disease.

65.

If you fall, you won't be able to get back up.*

*Maybe a good-looking stranger will help you to your feet.

66.

Complaining will become a favorite pastime.*

*Someone needs to keep track of all the things that are wrong with the world today.

67.

You won't want to stay out late anymore.*

*You won't be able to stay up late either.

68.

You'll wake up at the crack of dawn.*

*And fall asleep shortly after sunset.

69.

Your perfect posture will disappear and you'll stoop.*

*After a lifetime of standing up straight, isn't it relaxing to slouch?

70.

You'll be stuck in the past.*

*You can say "back in my day" with aplomb.

71.

Bridge will become your biggest vice.*

*It's better than gambling.

72.

You'll turn into your parents.*

*You probably already have.

73.

That old person
smell will be
coming from you.*

*Great excuse to buy new perfume.

74.

Some cool new technology will be invented—and you'll miss out on it.*

*Don't worry, you wouldn't be able to understand it anyway.

75.

You'll get crow's-feet.*

*You'll look distinguished.

76.

Nobody wants to see an old lady in a miniskirt.*

*Hey, if you've got it, flaunt it.

77.

Nobody wants to
see an old man in a
banana hammock.*

*Hey, if you've got it, flaunt it.

78.

You'll move to Florida, like all the other geezers.*

*Tanned sagging flesh is better
than pale sagging flesh.

79.

Some con man will swindle you out of your retirement savings.*

*You'll learn some great budgeting skills.

80.

You'll wear comfortable shoes.*

*At the end of a long day,
your dogs won't be barking.

81.

No one will
flirt with you.*

*Finally, you can walk down the street in peace.

82.

You haven't done everything on your bucket list yet.*

*There's no time like the present.

83.

You won't know how
to fill your days
once you retire.*

*You'll have ample time to write that book.
Or catch up on some sleep.

84.

Making out a will is a pain.*

*You can punish those who've wronged you.

85.

Taking the stairs will be physically impossible.*

*You won't get dirty looks for
taking the elevator one floor up.

Your days of traveling the world will be over.*

*You can watch travel shows.
It's basically the same thing.

87.

Your eyesight will go.*

*You won't notice that layer of dust
on your crystal figurine collection.

88.

Your hearing will go.*

*All those loud bars? No longer a problem.

89.

You'll be forced to contemplate your own mortality.*

*It's inevitable. Unless you're a cyborg.

Someone, someday, is going to call you "Grandpa."*

*You'll get all the fun of kids again—
but only the toy-buying part!

91.

You'll be invisible.*

*You can stop trying so hard.

92.

You won't know what the cool slang is.*

*Use the slang from your youth.
Everything old is new again!

93.

You might not ever find "the one."*

*Plenty of people claim they did—and divorced.

94.

The future will be amazing, and you're going to miss it.*

*But you won't have to worry about the apocalypse.

95.

You'll be the oldest one at the gym.*

*But not at the gerontologist.

96.

Age spots will replace acne.*

*They're just like freckles, but supersized.

97.

Celebrating your birthday will just bum you out.*

*You're giving age the middle finger!

98.

You'll have to get new body parts.*

*Isn't that better than used body parts?

99.

You'll run out
of time.*

*If that's true, you can probably
quit cleaning behind furniture.

100.

You'll forget important names and dates.*

*Wait, what were you saying?

*Don't worry.
It happens to
all of us.

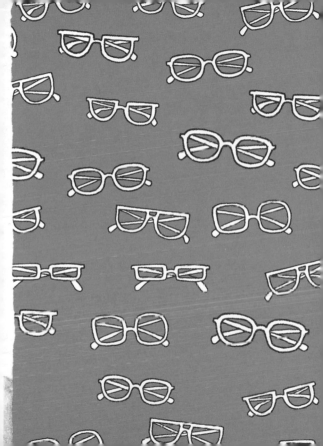

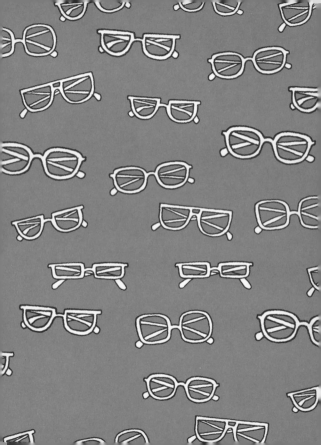